Taking Care of Me

Taking Care of Me

TODAY, TOMORROW, FOR A LIFETIME

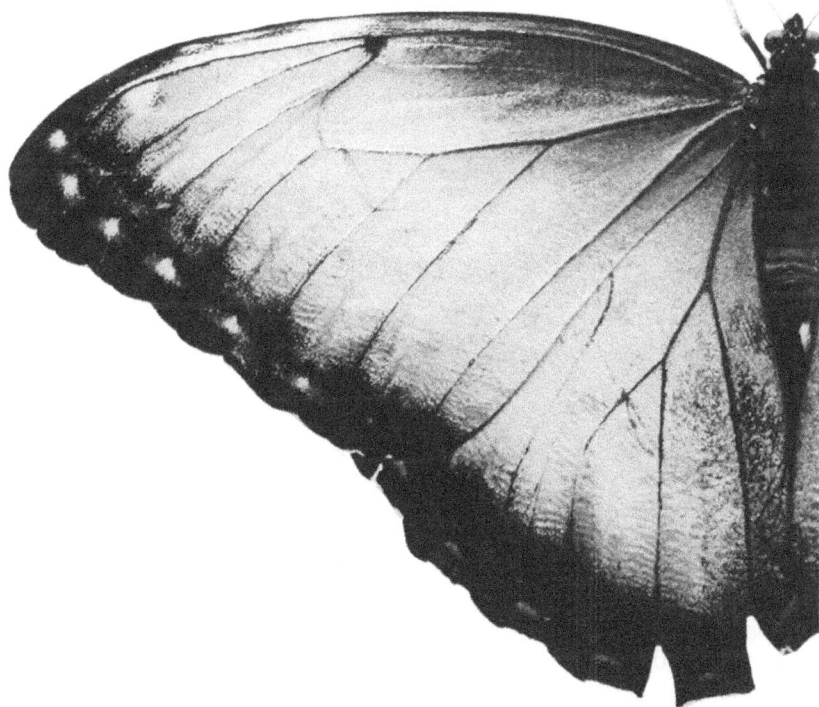

Teresa Lynn Todd Payne

credo

house publishers

Published in the United States of America by Credo House Publishers,
a division of Credo Communications, LLC, Grand Rapids, Michigan
credohousepublishers.com

ISBN: 978-1-62586-227-3

Cover design and interior typesetting by Believe Book Design LLC
Editing by Donna Huisjen

Printed in the United States of America
First edition

Contents

Preface

(Today, Tomorrow, for a Lifetime)

TAKING CARE OF ME TODAY

Oftentimes people today, whether they're, rich or poor, teenagers, college students, single adults, parents, partners, or grandparents, don't take time out for themselves. We're so busy taking care of others, helping one another, working, or going to school, . . . and for some of us, we are just trying to figure out what our next step will be or how we got to where we are right now. At this very moment in time, there's someone each of us knows who is trying to figure out the answer to different life circumstances and to What do I do now? At this very moment in time, there's someone who is lost in the darkness and is seeking the Light of the World, our Lord and Savior, our Heavenly Father, for direction and guidance. At this very moment in time, there's someone who is hurting, whose life has been turned upside down. At this very moment in time, there's someone who is searching for her soulmate, someone who has found and married her best friend, and someone who has yet to understand that to love someone else means you have to start by loving yourself. At this very moment in time, there's someone who is living their life to the fullest, who is living their life for Christ, who is living out their goals and aspirations but doesn't stop dreaming. At this very moment in time, someone is looking at the world around them and questioning why things are the way they are. The list of circumstances goes on, but, at this very moment in time, one must live for today and know that our hope and strength for tomorrow comes from the Lord.

TAKING CARE OF ME TOMORROW

TOMORROW IS A BLESSING—AN OPPORTUNITY AND RENEWAL, AN EXTENSION OF THE DAY YOU LIVED TODAY. HOW WILL YOU CHOOSE TO LIVE?

If given tomorrow, how will you choose to live? What, if anything, will you do differently? Who will you live for? Taking Care of Me: Tomorrow is about searching your soul. It's about examining ourselves and all that God created us to be. It's about knowing that the tears we shed in good times and bad and the cry of our hearts are not to be shunned or viewed as signs of weakness; instead, they are a signal of humanity, humility, and strength. It is our tears and life experiences that help us grow and keep us growing and becoming more resilient, with the aid of God's unchanging hand that holds us up just when we think we're going it alone. It's our ability to laugh at ourselves that makes us human. It's our desire to share our joys and challenges with those we love that helps breed trust, security, hope, and happiness. It's breaking those unhealthy habits, cutting short the cycle of clinging to those empty things and destructive relationships that will help us become women of strength. Tomorrow is about you. If given tomorrow, what will you do? Each day is a new gift, an opportunity for self-reflection, for thinking ahead before your feet even hit the floor in the morning. So, before you close your eyes to rest, and as you rise tomorrow to get out of bed, . . . pause. Just pause. Give thanks. Count your blessings for yesterday, share your hopes and dreams for tomorrow, and go for it by any means necessary. You deserve nothing less than everything you hope for and are destined to be.

TAKING CARE OF ME FOR A LIFETIME

Whoo, Wee. If only we could know what tomorrow holds; if only we could know now what we'll know then. If only we could rewind the clock, fall back for real—for real! I'm sure there's a thing or two we might all want a do over again or things we may want to do more of. There are people we'll wish we could have spent more time with, to take the time and truly be present. If only we could fast-forward through life to see where our paths may lead. If only I really wanted all my paths to be straightforward like that, . . . but I don't. For my path (maybe like yours) has included some curves, bumps, and a few roundabouts but no matter the path in life, I've learned that you can find strength and joy in the journey.

Taking Care of Me: for a Lifetime . . . is just that. Take Care, my friends. Because it's not just about me. It's about you! Yeah, You! It's about every moment in your life, every person you have met or will meet, every relationship you have built or will build with someone, every friendship you have or will cherish, the relationships that you have mended, and the ones that have been broken. It's about the questions you have asked or will ask, the decisions you have made or will make, the memories and experiences that have helped shape who you are today—and the ones that will shape tomorrow and the rest of your life. It's about the good times, hard times, sad times, fun times, and even the having-the-time-of-your-life kinds of times. I know that's a whole lot of times, but that's what happens in your own personal journey to Taking Care of YOU: for a Lifetime.

I have been shaped and reshaped by every experience in my life. We are all more alike than we are different. As I bring this collection of poetry and writings to you today, I'm beginning to write my full story in song: who I am and what I've gone through, my sacrifices, my endurance, and my strength to be a Woman of God's design. Through it all, take care, ya'll. Trust me when I say that, through it all, **I Am. I Am Beautiful. I Am Strong. I Am Able. I Am Resilient. I Am Hopeful. I Am Love. I Am a Child of God.** To everyone who has played a significant and positive role in my life, thank you. Everything that God has yet in store for me in my lifetime I will receive with open arms, giving thanks. And so, my friends, Take Care of You for a Lifetime because **You Deserve All The Happiness.** Extend your arms wide and get ready to embrace all the goodness, blessings, and gifts that are within reach in your lifetime. Let's Get It!

Chapter One

MY DWELLING PLACE

To dwell is to find that place
That special person, experience, or situation to embrace.
Some dwell in the comfort of their own being
While others find their dwelling place in sacrificing themselves
For evil doings of the world that yield only temporary satisfaction.

To be in a state of smug complacency
Is like losing the ground beneath your feet;
Without something solid to stand on
You give way to any unordinary circumstance
That comes to rest at your stoop.

Some dwell in the homes of others
For they have no place of their own to go
Making no plans for their next destination
Settling as the roots beneath their feet begin to grow.

Some dwell in the homes of others
Where the young and innocent sleep
Mindless of any negative influence
That may run in the soul so deep.

Dwellers dwell for a reason
Some because they have no place to go
In need of food, warmth, and shelter
A place to deal with what life throws.

Some obtain their dwelling with deception
Driven by living their life without you;
Taking steps with selfish intent is not true love
Just look at the hurt they cause you.

Some dwell on old memories
Holding onto times from the past
Attempting to weasel their way back into your life
With empty words, broken promises, day-old talk, and trash.

People try to dwell in your heart
Despite all they have done
Envy and jealousy—roots of evil—
Shake your spirit while striving to function as one.

For some a dwelling place is an establishment
A worldly relationship with a woman or man
Not even built by God's design
But built with a grain of sand.

A true dwelling puts God at the center of two hearts
Holding strong onto one another's hands
Providing a firm foundation from the start.

People feel stuck with others dwelling
From day to day
Moving without direction
Doing and saying devoid of discretion.
May God have mercy on their souls and forgive them for transgressions.

To dwell is not only to be who you are
        But to be who you are in Christ;
To dwell is to not only be in the house of the Lord
        But to keep the Lord in your house;
To dwell is not only to be with the one you love
        But to love as Christ loved and hold on for dear life.

IN THE STORM

I'm caught in the midst of a storm
A stronghold between trying to do something right
And displaced perceptions of doing wrong,

Anxious to please and ready to be kind
Genuine at heart—all qualities of mine.

The storm is brewing with thoughtless words
Actions from pent-up emotion
Feelings stemming from bearing others' burdens
Become a real frustration.

Shielded from our deepest thought
From bearing the unrest that's wrought
The storm of the day-to-day events unfolds
Descends into a downward spiral.

At the core one can see the meanings of good deeds:
To bring out joy or accentuate the positive
To come out of the storm to examine the roots
To see if the dirt sticks or if it falls off
To see if you find a blessing, a teaching moment,
To find opportunity, something to give thanks for . . .

While in the midst of a storm
The thunder will still roar
The rain will still come down
The wind will still blow.

We know everything happens for a reason
And only God knows what he spares us from
In the storm, whatever it may be,
Every plant, every creature—even me—
Needs watering, a little sun,
And a whole lot of love . . . in the storm.

IT'S RAINING

The wind is blowing
The rain begins to fall
The lightning flashes
The thunder calls
The wind is whipping
It's storming now;
Please let us in—it's cold out, ya'll.

People are starving every day
We throw away food versus giving it away
We complain that we have nothing to wear
While people are clothed in rags with tears.
People are struggling to make ends meet
Hoping to keep food on the table until next week
While others are concerned with keeping on the heat
Some are just longing to get off the street.
The wind is blowing
The rain begins to fall
The lightning flashes
The thunder calls
The wind is whipping
It's storming now;
Please let us in—it's cold out, ya'll.

Men and women out searching for jobs
Wishing and praying and questioning God
Rejections abound—will we catch a break
Will someone give us a chance
Or continue to compound the unemployment rate?
The wind is blowing
The rain begins to fall
The lightning flashes
The thunder calls
The wind is whipping
It's storming now;
Please let us in—it's cold out, ya'll.

Our kids are dying every day
From stupid murders and thoughtless acts
What will it take to get our youth back?
Too much is drugs, so much is pride
So much is a sense of hopelessness
No models or guides.
The wind is blowing
The rain begins to fall
The lightning flashes
The thunder calls
The wind is whipping
It's storming now;
Please let us in—it's cold out, ya'll.

Selling drugs to make some cheddar
Willing to forego on making life better
Selling bodies and assets just for a high
Stealing from loved ones
Breaking family ties.
The wind is blowing
The rain begins to fall
The lightning flashes
The thunder calls
The wind is whipping
It's storming now;
Please let us in—it's cold out, ya'll.

Walking around in a zombie-like state
Lost and afraid, awaiting one's fate—
Unknown futures, shattered dreams,
Sacrificing self as the Man grins and gleans
Taking all from you till nothing is left
Only what feels like a ton of bricks
Weighing down on your chest
As you fight to catch what may be your last breath
Or stand up to calculate what to do next.
The wind is blowing
The rain begins to fall

The lightning flashes
The thunder calls
The wind is whipping
It's storming now;
Please let us in—it's cold out, ya'll.

Many live in districts of deprivation
Or dwell in homes with lead infestation
Or challenged by high-interest mortgage rates
And buried in debt
Or striving to meet the basic needs
Or can't afford to pay the rent.
The wind is blowing
The rain begins to fall
The lightning flashes
The thunder calls
The wind is whipping
It's storming now;
Please let us in—it's cold out, ya'll.

Where are some of our men, the fathers and boys?
And women, the mothers and girls?
Families robbed; populations destroyed
Trying to keep it together but left with a void:
Absenteeism, societal stress
Lack of opportunities, survival, and thriving
Due to broken systems and mess
Overrepresentation by design
In the prison industrial complex.
The wind is blowing
The rain begins to fall
The lightning flashes
The thunder calls
The wind is whipping
It's storming now;
Please let us in—it's cold out, ya'll.

Waiting and waiting to finally get out
Stripped of identity
Acquiring self-doubt—
The day comes and you're finally free
But motionless and captured
Now where is that key?
The wind is blowing
The rain begins to fall
The lightning flashes
The thunder calls
The wind is whipping
It's storming now;
Please let us in—it's cold out, ya'll.

People try to move forward to stay on the track
But oppression and stressors press down, hold them back
The cycle of evil still cyclones around
Young girls having babies, with love never found
The schools and the systems fail youth every day
Promoting too soon—what will youth take away?
The wind is blowing
The rain begins to fall
The lightning flashes
The thunder calls
The wind is whipping
It's storming now;
Please let us in—it's cold out, ya'll.

Our nation is sick, getting sicker each day
Health care so much more than ability to pay
Medicare, Medicaid,
No Insurance, Private Pay
Poor diet, the sedentary lifestyles we lead
A lack of fresh air and green spaces we need
Lack of access, so many obstructions to care—
Organize and take action; make sure you're aware!
The wind is blowing
The rain begins to fall

Taking Care of Me

The lightning flashes
The thunder calls
The wind is whipping
It's storming now;
Please let us in—it's cold out, ya'll.

Bridging gaps in health disparity—what will it take?
To live free of pain and not assume one's fate.
Whether it's cancer, HIV/AIDS, diabetes
Hypertension, high cholesterol, obesity
Heart disease, Crohn's disease, lupus, stroke
Sickle cell anemia, gout, or conditions of secondhand smoke.
Whether it's alcoholism, asthma, glaucoma
Emphysema, bronchitis, pneumonia
Flu symptoms or a cough you can't shake
Or those new emerging viruses
More challenging to escape.
The wind is blowing
The rain begins to fall
The lightning flashes
The thunder calls
The wind is whipping
It's storming now;
Please let us in—it's cold out, ya'll.

Multiple problems and chronic disease
Only One knows your battles
That One holds the key—
All we are to do is have faith and believe.

God rules o'er this world and can handle it all
God stops the rain before it can fall
God holds the lightning and thunder in place
It's God in the wind we feel brush past our face.
When the storm comes, take shelter where you can
But the best spot to be is in the cleft of His hand.

Teresa Lynn Payne

WHY DID I CRY TODAY?

I awoke with the rising of the sun
But couldn't grasp a new day had begun.

As I lay in the bed, glistening light in my eyes
I felt that dead weight and knew I might cry.

Why did I cry? I do not know . . .
The pressure of carrying a heavy load?

Why must I bear this daunting luggage of mine?
Shouldn't I give it to my Lord Divine—
The pain, the hurt, the loss within?
Then why did I wake with a frown, not a grin?

The dreams we have, that unexplored source
That drives our emotions with uncontained force

No thought or pattern comes to mind
Like balled-up yarn you try to unwind,

There's just no unraveling what is for real
Perceptions are skewed by whatever we feel.

If only I'd asked my God to release
The worries that bind me, that sit on my back
Given way to our Father to unpack my sack . . .

He sees the mist, puts the storms at bay
And so, I ask God, WHY DID I CRY TODAY?

Chapter Two

BROKEN

To be broke is simply to have nothing left
Unable to make something the way it was before.
It doesn't matter the number of pieces
It doesn't matter the elements or objects
It doesn't matter the type or color
Not even if it's quiet or makes noise
If it's ugly or beautiful—rich or poor.

Broken requires two pieces, not one
Each designed to fit within the other
Never intended to come undone.
Broken's a state in which something exists
Awaiting an outcome—Is there a fix?
A fix isn't easy without all the parts
You want to reorder but don't know where to start.

Some give up right off the cuff
Revert to the same old way
Glossing over the cracks just as though
Yesterday were today.

Some feel despair, don't want to face what's real
Others pray and patiently wait to see what God reveals.

Add to a broken part, the spirit of brokenness
Plus, the underlying meaning and depth that brings the
conditions or degrees of tests.

To see yourself as the broken part
Or the part that no longer fits
Is to answer the pertinent question:
Should you try again or quit?

Whether you are the one did the breaking
Or the one who's just plain broke,
Stop making withdrawals, deposit instead
Try singing a different note
Walk to the beat of a different drum
Try an approach brand new
Make something right for yourself and your life
Do whatever it is you can do.

If you try and it still doesn't work
At least you know you tried—
Maybe the part that's missing
Is no longer fitting for you or wise.

Broken parts or pieces
Small remnants and remains
God has a way and plans for all
Though we may never be the same.
We don't always know why things may break
Or whether we'll have what it takes
To be part of a whole or continue alone
Let's just let God smooth out our edges
To polish us up like a beautiful stone.

We can talk about broken objects
We can talk about broken parts
But when the SOUL learns BROKENNESS
This is where God imparts:

Infusions of His love and care
Joy when we feel sorrow
Provision of comfort and fuel for today
Hope and promise for tomorrow.

ROLL WITH THE PUNCHES

Sometimes you must roll with the punches
You never know what the next curve ball will be;
Put on your glove and catcher's mitt
Prepare for the pop fly you see.

To take a punch here or there
No matter if no one's aware,
Keeping matters to yourself
Is like opening an unread book
And placing it back on the shelf.

Leaving things unsaid
Not finishing a broken mend
Listening with a deaf ear
Is like a jarring clang that is not clear.

Standing behind the walls of destruction
Eager to make a new life that's constructive
What do you say?
What do you do?
Keep things bottled up or be on your way?

Search your soul
Examine your heart
Discern your thoughts and feelings
Before you make a start.

Pray and wait with patience
For God to act or move
Don't look to left or right
Or up or down to take your clue.

God is the all-loving God
Who answers every prayer
So never underestimate
His plans and realm of care.

Jesus is a receiver
An interceptor of God's will
To take our worries and burdens on Him
To bring peace and make us still

He focuses our minds and lenses
So, we may clearly see
Jesus as our point guard
Ever so gently guiding you and me
In the right direction
Down a different road
Where we don't have to roll with the punches
Or whatever life may throw;
So choose to live for Jesus
And let Him carry your load!

Teresa Lynn Payne

THE SLAP SHOT

HE SLAPPED ME IN THE FACE AND PUNCHED ME IN THE GUT

I have never really been slapped in the face or punched in the gut
So how could I know that it would hurt so much?
The sting on my face was from what I could see
I knew something wasn't right, but what could it be?

My face was flushed, uncertainty set in
I was formulating questions and thoughts within;

My heart was racing, my face grew warm,
My blood was hot, my heart was torn.

I was there to be supportive, helpful, and kind
Yet clueless how things would start to unwind.

It was like the slap of a hand across my face
I was there in the darkness
Wanting something to embrace.

For all I had thought to be true,
To my dismay,
Was revealed to be falsehood when
Two lives crossed paths one day.

I felt my knees buckle
I thought I couldn't take it,
But I smiled at those around me—
Somehow, some way, I faked it.

I could feel my spirit move me,
Felt a stirring deep inside,
As I groped to find my fit,
For my place in this grave time.

Taking Care of Me

This once familiar face,
Thought a person of integrity,
Now suddenly utterly foreign to me—

The voice I heard barking
The questions she posed:
Who was she to ask me?
My own lips were closed.

My head was pounding from the blow
This jolt upon my mind,
Felt pushed aside, kicked down, thrust off,
My stomach in a bind.

Oh, the secrets clearly allowed to persist
That allowed one to act like I don't exist.

I was raised better than not to be known
For I'm a strong woman, as history has shown.

I will bounce back from a slap or a hit.
The sting will fade quickly if the facts do not fit.

But to have the wind knocked from you,
Still an ordeal
To be bowed from a "gut-punch"
That felt oh, so real.

My breathing was rapid,
A catch in my throat,
I had to leave quickly,
Take it in while remote.

I strolled down the length of a long corridor
Closing that chapter with hospital door.

The tears rolled unhindered; I felt all alone,
Yet my Comforter held me that night when at home.

Teresa Lynn Payne

Could I count as a blessing the lessons I'd learned?
When in tribulation, they're hard to discern.

I've never been slapped, never punched in the gut,
But this rock in my heart, what a hard one to cut!

I had to allow myself freedom to feel
The anger and hurt and to take time to heal.

I've long set about to be a good friend
To support, to defend, to mend and to lend,

But the time came to question, be straight and direct,
To contemplate, figure out what would be next.

I searched for an answer, a change in perspective,
A credible comeback, convincing corrective.

Denial eludes me, and lack of recall
Just doesn't equate to Nothing happened at all.

I mean, just who do you think that I am?
I say what's required, and I do what I can.

But I refuse to give up one more moment of time
To hide in a web of lies long intertwined.

Why waste more time not letting go of the past?
I know who I am in Christ—that truth will last!

I will move on to bright days, new memories made—
For He tells me I'm lovely, not for show or display.

You can't take me out, put me back any day,
Like a broom you use briefly to sweep dirt away.

I deserve better, so this Slap Shot's on you!

And so, my friends, don't second-guess, fret, or stew.
Stand up and dispute—it feels good when you do.

When you do what is right and try to stay true
Know that your Father is right there with you.

A person may score with their first slap shot, but it's not the slap shot that wins this game in life, but the goalie that prevents the slap shot from happening again or entering your life in the first place—now that's a winner. Play games with me and you'll surely lose.

—Teresa Lynn

THE POWER TO BE

You have the power to be
Any and everything you desire indeed
You have the power to excel.
Work hard and be diligent so others can tell.
You have the power to embrace
All your goals and dreams at your determined pace.
You have the power and might
To stand tall amongst others without shame or fright.
You have the power to overcome
All obstacles and challenges based on victories won.
You have the power to move ahead—
Always speak up and leave nothing unsaid.
You have the power to explore
Release inhibitions—allow yourself to soar,
You have the power to exercise your rights
Stand up for what you believe and fight.
You have the power to voice your concern
Grab leaders' attention—help others to learn.
You have the power to be free—
Work for yourself and support communities in need.
You have the power to use your mind
To plan the course, you hope to find.
You have the power to care
Lend help to others everywhere.
You have the power to be a friend
Always available till the end.
You have the power to do
Any task, job, or career in front of you.
You have the power to create
Visions and programs to improve others' state.
You have the power to let your light shine—
No permission is needed—You're one of a kind.
You have the power to not be confined
By constructs or barriers that seek to define.
You have the power to not be content
Keep growing and learning with strong self-intent.

You have the power to lead
Seek to acquire the skills that you'll need.
You have the power to speak
Lift your voice—don't be weak.
You have the power to feel
All emotions that make people real.

You have the power to be:
        Who you are
        Where you are
        Whoever you're with
        Whenever you want
        Whatever you do and
        Everywhere you go
Know that people know that we—you and
I—are powerful beyond measure.

Power is a wonderful thing when intentions of exercising power stem from your heart, mind and soul and don't cause harm to others but help you become all that you can be. Now that's POWER in practice.

—Teresa Lynn

WORDS IN THOUGHT

Thoughts are the root cause of our actions
Propelling us forward to a desired outcome
In order to keep us grounded
Allowing one to decipher right from wrong, good from bad,
Positive from negative, just from unjust or
Other parallels that invite a stance.

Thoughts put into action can lead to destruction
Or guide a group to new construction
Spoken thoughts can begin or end a dialogue,
Confrontation, or conversation
Words spoken with tact and careful thought
Lead to conscious persuasion.

Careless thoughts spoken can't be unsaid.
Be cautious proceeding and choose words ahead—
Choose words that fit well the backdrop or condition—
Considering context, use tactful admonition.

Always speak up with words that cannot be misconstrued.
Draw from thoughts and experiences intrinsic to you.

Tell stories and visions with words steeped in thought
To bring about change in a world that's distraught.

Words are just words spoken in isolation
But words that deliver a message can inspire
And produce an effect in a bleak situation.

Words can be demeaning
Or words can uplift
But the greatest Word that ever existed
Was brought to us as God's gift.

Taking Care of Me

As scary and nerve-wracking as it is to speak your mind
Search for just the right words with no need to rewind.

Take the Word as it is—
Don't infer, mince, or splice it.
Apply the only Word to life
And, seeking Truth, you'll find it.

Chapter Three

YOUNG WOMEN, YOUNG LIVES

Young Women, Young Lives,
Spirit of Young Minds,
Desperately searching for love and affection
Journeying onward in quest of connection,

Pieces of hope,
Shattered dreams
Look in the wrong places
To mend broken seams,

Trudging down that endless road
Bearing your burden and hefting your load,
Life's stressors set in, causing challenge to cope.

Fearful of seeing what may lie ahead
Side-stepping or skirting, back-tracking instead,
Making U-turns and avoiding the curves—
Learn to read between lines
and to question the words.

For words without thought are so much rambling talk
But words prompting action prepare you to walk—

Taking Care of Me

To take steps in the right direction
Keeping your head up in quest of perfection.

To be the beautiful soul God designed you to be
Is to overcome obstacles there on your journey,

Learning and growing each step of the way
Through struggles and setbacks, through trials and dismay,
Remember things stem from your choice and God's plan
His Spirit enables, backs up your "I can."

So cast yourself in a more positive light—
Emerge from the shadows, put darkness to flight,
To draw from strengths settled down deep in your heart,
To develop your assets, to do your best part,
Take action, be candid, direct, and forthright.
Direct your feet forward, goals ever in sight.

Focus on what you desire to achieve
Examine your heart, mind, and soul—just believe,
Concentrate on accomplishments, less on rewards
Put your trust in God above, thank the Lord
For He made each one, and He opens our doors.

Serve Him as a woman of God; know your worth—
One day you will dance with Him on His new earth,
Young Women, Young Lives, . . . Spirit of Young Minds.

ON BEING THERE

It's not how often you talk that makes the difference in life.

What matters is their knowing you're always right there
Because you always have been.

Your mutual knowing how to reach out to one another
Because you know when you need to.

Their knowing what you're thinking without a spoken word
Just because you know them like that.

Your mutual knowing that each of you will be there when you're overjoyed
And when it feels like everything around you is crumbling down
Just because you want to.

It's not how often you talk that makes the difference in life.

What counts is how much you listen, how much you
hear, how much you care, how much you love, how
much you share, how often you're there . . .

When your Sistahs need you.

TAKING RISK—FOR MY SISTAHS

"When we come to the edge of the light we know and are about to step off into the darkness of the unknown, of this we can be sure . . . either God will provide something solid to stand on or we will be taught to fly."—Unknown

It's time to soar, it's time to fly
Pick up the pace, or life shall pass you by.

It's time to soar, it's time to fly
Life lacks rhyme or reason, yet always ask why.

It's time to soar, it's time to fly
Set achievable goals and always aim high.

It's time to soar, it's time to fly
Pack your bag and say goodbye.

It's time to soar, it's time to fly
Stop looking back at what you left behind.

It's time to soar, it's time to fly
Do not worry: God's at your side.

It's time to soar, it's time to fly
Don't settle for less—Where is your pride?

It's time to soar, it's time to fly
Don't go it alone, let God be your guide.

It's time to soar, it's time to fly
Stop holding back, take bigger strides.

It's time to soar, it's time to fly
Go for your dreams and reach for the sky.

It's time to soar, it's time to fly
Don't be afraid, let go and unwind.

It's time to soar, it's time to fly
Embrace your close friends and help them to rise.

It's time to soar, it's time to fly
Do something new, try it on for size.

It's time to soar, it's time to fly
Let your journey begin after a good cry.

It's time to soar, it's time to fly
Open your arms, stretch them out wide.

It's time to soar, it's time to fly
Don't wait for a special occasion—
     Just Fly, Fly, Fly!

MY PALE YELLOW DRESS

(MY LITTLE BLACK DRESS IS YELLOW)

I want to buy that pale yellow dress,
The one that I saw in the storefront window.

I want to try on that pale yellow dress—
The one with capped sleeves, trimming waistline, flowing bottom—
Because yellow is one of my favorite colors, you know.

I want to stand by a mirror to see that pale yellow dress,
The one with a scooped neckline, and wear glistening accessories
to dangle from my ears and embrace my neck, with elegant, yet
dainty shoes fit to show at the hem.

In that pale yellow dress, I want to pull my hair back in a swoop
and let a few curls fall onto my shoulders as I look from side to side.

I want to buy that pale yellow dress because it's just perfect for me.
It's not lacy or frilly, too long, short, or tight.
It looks fun, simple, daring—unique and just right!

I want to take home that pale yellow dress
The one that I saw in the storefront window;
To go to a place I can sing, dance, and twirl,
Be swept off my feet and lost in time.

I want to wear that pale yellow dress as I walk into a room
To show that the beauty is Not in the dress—
it's through me His light exudes.

The garment is just a yellow dress, although I love it so
It doesn't make me who I am, . . . nor does it even know.

The dress and accessories will go out of style
And material interests in are never worthwhile.

Teresa Lynn Payne

You make authentic statements through what you do and say—
People need to notice you . . . not the dress you wear today.

It's not only about the yellow dress;
It's learning to walk with confidence.

It's not only about the dainty shoes
But about how you step and Who's guiding you.

It's not only about accessories
But helping others and aiming to please.

It's not only about music or dancing to song
But giving to others, making right from wrong.

It's not about the yellow dress—
So, stand up and trust God through all of life's tests.

Whenever you put on your pale-yellow dress—
Whether old or borrowed or new—
Try on one of these thoughts, or maybe two:
As a woman of God, be your best, true to you!

Chapter Four

MY HEART, MY JOY, MY SOUL

My, My, My Denny and Shay
Years just keep passing me by.

Time does not stop
For me or for you
Remembering days as though yesterday
Rocking and holding you.

As newborn babes
One quiet and still
The other vivacious, all cries, laughs, and thrills.

Day by day
Watching you grow
Watching you sleep and awake
Each moment cherished
Through goodness and sadness and little mistakes,

Through growth and opportunity
Loving you, laughing with you,
Crying my tears
Through celebrations, milestones, and birthday years.

Taking Care of Me

You've managed to do so well
Despite disruptions, adversity, trials
Skills you've mastered already in life
Will help you succeed and soar on through the miles.

Taught to love the Lord, always quick to forgive
Even eager to love me through parenting woes—
Just loving me because I am Momma.

Children with hearts of gold
You are my heart, my joy, you are my soul . . . My, My, My.

REFLECTIONS

I see me in you;
Although we're not tied through family or blood
There's something familiar
Not fully understood.

From two distinct places
Have two women come
Rooted in similar values:
Strong family upbringings
That won't be undone.

Two different pathways
Two different lives
Two educated sisters
One's searching for answers
The other knows why.

I see your struggle
I sense your concern
Self-doubt enters in
Makes it hard to discern

What decisions to make
What now lies ahead.
Your needs secondary—
Kids' welfare instead.

How natural this thing that as mothers we do:
Look first to their interest,
Then look out for you

But know it's okay to do something for you
Once you accept you did all that you could do.

Taking Care of Me

In going forward, whatever you do,
Keep the young ones close at heart.
Give them honesty and love—
Surely, they won't depart.

THE WELLSPRING

This is a short story, a wellspring of life.

A wellspring that tells of a daughter's and a mother's love for each other and love for life. A wellspring bears the fountain of life, a water source to share. For in our souls, we each are the host of a wellspring of tears that bring forth and bear—sometimes knowingly, though at times unaware.

From earliest days came my daughter's soft cry into this world—so astounded was I to watch her grow in the early years, falling off her bike—me observing the tears. To the tears in my eyes as she parted my side to begin daycare with other small children her size. To the times I would stay up late to comfort her when sick or afraid. She has a wellspring in her mother, each in tune like the beat of a drum to the other. For when she laughs it makes me smile, and when she cries I mourn with her for a while. When she walks in the room, I can see her light shine to help and love others—a shared passion of mine. We sing to different tunes but stay in tune with one another. We dance and shout to different music, but we get down and know how to jam. She shows me new moves, but I taught this child of mine how to groove. She constantly tells me to turn off my blinker, but I will always drive her in the right direction. For she is *my* wellspring, though from me she came. Born of me, she has made me change. Different taste with her own unique styles and flair, yet digs in my closet for something to wear. Like her mother's, her soft voice exudes strength and might; don't push us around—let me warn you, we'll fight! She's gifted, creative right down to the core, I look forward to seeing all God has in store. She's a blessing by God's design, part of my fabric—we're that intertwined.

Whenever she calls, I'm right there; night or day I'm there for my daughter and friend, for my Shay (I call her Felisha).
—Love, Ma (She calls me Felicity)

ON GIVING THANKS

Thanks be to those
Who give of themselves to others.

Thanks be to you
For outstretched arms when someone's in need.

What a wonderful demonstration
When one shows care through random acts of kindness

But what a blessing indeed
When one displays actions as a child of God:

What a wonderful reflection of God's work in your soul.

ON GOING HOME

I'm homebound,
The distance is the only thing that separates me from home.

I can see the door open to me
Swinging back and forth
Awaiting my arrival.

The fresh and soulful aromas
Arise in the kitchen
Ma's stirring the pots
Da's napping, reading, or plundering.

Can't you see their smiles?
Can't you hear their voices?
You can feel home's presence
As the car tires hit the pavement with force.

Entering the driveway
Can't get inside fast enough
Ready to give love and feel embraced
Ready to laugh and share stories
To see my reflection upon their face.

There's something about going home
It's comfortable and all is at ease
No matter what, you can be yourself,
Happy and carefree.

For this is a warm place
One open to all who stop by
Where generosity flows from the heart
Creating challenges for family and friends to depart.

Sleeping in is so wonderful here
Rest is plentiful and serene
Just lie back and relax on the front porch
Kick up your feet
Close your eyes and dream.
Of course, there are sounds around you
As it wouldn't be home without the noise
Crickets chirping, frogs croaking
People talking, music blasting
While kids play with their toys.

It's amazing how all things come forth in unison
All from within one home
The fabric of my being
My Da has planted, my Ma has sewn.

I'm homebound
Outside of heaven,
Going home is one of the best places to be
Sitting around the kitchen table with family
Eating, talking, and joking merrily.

Playing games together
Spending quality time
Learning family history
Through the latest genealogy research Da finds.

You never grow bored here
There's always something to do
If you can't find that something
That something or work will find you.

God is clearly present here
Without Him we'd begin to roam
For He knows the roads we travel on
And the pathway that leads us back home.

Chapter Five

COME WALK WITH ME

Where are you walking?
    Do you even know where?
Where are you walking?
    Do you even care?

Where are you walking?
    Do you even know why?
Where are you walking?
    Are you willing to try?

Where are you walking?
    Do you know where this path leads?
Where are you walking?
    Do you know what you need?

Where are you walking?
    Do you feel okay?
Where are you walking?
    Who's leading the way?

Where are you walking?
    Clear vision in sight?
Where are you walking?
    In darkness or light?

Where are you walking?
    Do you need me to go?
Where are you walking?
    Do you not even know?

Where are you walking?
    How long will it take?
Where are you walking?
    Are you willing to wait?

Where are you walking?
    Are you prepared to walk?
Where are you walking?
    Are you all about talk?

Where are you walking?
    Do you plan ahead each step?
Where are you walking?
    Do you know what's next?

Where are you walking?
    Do you know desire within?
Where are you walking?
    Are you hanging on a limb?

Where are you walking?
    Do you frequently look back?
Where are you walking?
    Is it slow or is it fast?

Where are you walking?
    Do you know whom to trust?
Where are you walking?
    Do you do what you must?

Where are you walking?
    Do you know just what to do?
Where are you walking?
    Want me to pray for you?

Where are you walking?
    Do you ever feel the doubt?
Where are you walking?
    Need to take a different route?

Where are you walking?
    Looked for guidance from above?
Where are you walking?
    Know God's presence and His love?

Where are you walking?
    Are you willing to take a stand?
Where are you walking?
    Who's that holding your hand?

LIFE IS LIKE A NEW JOURNEY, A CONTINUOUS CYCLE OF LEARNING ALONG THE WAY.

—Teresa Lynn

JESUS MY REDEEMER

Jesus, my Redeemer,
Save my soul
Purify me and make me whole
Take my hand and guide me so.
Bear my burdens
Lessen my load
Lead me down your trodden path
That I may see your love ever last.
Teach me Lord,
To do thy will
By making my walk with you
Not all downhill.
Lift me up
When I fall
Hear me, Lord,
Whenever I call.
Do that which is clear to you
Teach me to be kind and true.
Use me, Lord, to bring forth your Word
Eliminate thoughts that are absurd.
I am your vessel
Fill me up
Till goodness and blessings
Overrun my cup.
Take my hands
Stretch them out wide
That I may pour out my love
Built up inside
To reach other people
In need of a friend
Teaching them to lean on you, Jesus,
Whose love never ends.
Learning to trust in Jesus
Each step of the way
Giving thanks and praying fervently every day
Making room for God to light my path

That I may walk out of darkness and take off my mask
Revealing what is new in me
As God shines out with His divine beauty
That people may wonder and ask what they see
That I may respond: It's the good Lord in me.

Jesus, My Redeemer, will save your soul
He will purify you and make you whole.
The decision is yours—what will you do?
Take His hand now and He will lead you.

WHEN JESUS COMES

I wonder just how it will be
When our Lord and Savior comes for me.
Will I stand ready, prepared to go?
Or will I tremble with fright at the sight of His glow?

I wonder what you and I will do
When Jesus comes to make us new.
Will your arms be open to receive His grace
Or will you try to hide in shame and disgrace?

I wonder what will be the sound
As He rejoices in saved and lost souls found.
Will He truly sing over you and me
With an Almighty triumph for victory?

I wonder just what kind of place
God has for us when we finish our race
The beauty within those pearly gates
Of heaven and God's amazing grace.

I wonder at how patient God is
To wait on us to come to Him.
Are you still wandering, lost in sin,
Or will you accept Jesus and let Him in?

I wonder how far God's love will go:
He sent His only Son to die for us
To cover our sins with His blood.
Do you believe the blood of Christ was shed for you and me?
What an awesome sacrifice designed to set us free.

I wonder just How Great Thou Art
My God, in the light of all you've done:
Guiding us through storms, trials, and tribulations
Leading us in the right direction
To overcome worldly desires and temptation.

Teresa Lynn Payne

I wonder if I'll be able to speak
Or utter a verse from a song.
Will I be mute in silent awe or praise You all day long?
I can't imagine being left behind, so I'll keep my face to the Lord
Giving thanks and praying daily and adhering to the Word.

Chapter Six

RUNNERS, TAKE YOUR MARKS . . . SET . . . GO!

One should not be afraid to speak their mind
Or fear as a race nears the finish line.

One should feel free to openly share
To be on their mark every time, anywhere.

Relationships grow with good communication;
Runners wait for set command to get into motion.

Look ahead to see which way to go—
Runners who win don't just go with the flow.

When you find that special person who means so much to you
Anticipate the stretches of the race you must go through.

Without direction or a coach, it's hard to win a race;
You're running just to run, not even thinking of a place.

Some runners jump those hurdles, others run the straight-a-way;
Some sprint, some set a pace, run laps or miles, or legs of relays.

Taking Care of Me

In whatever the event a runner steps up to compete
Each knows the destination and the distance to complete.

Condition through the seasons; to the strategy pay heed;
I've yet to see one runner who refused to take the lead.

So, run with purpose, take a careful look at what's ahead
And spark communication; don't just
leave your thoughts unsaid.

If running with a purpose makes you feel a bit uneasy,
Ask the winner of a 400 if they feel a little queasy!

FREEDOM R.I.D.E.

Listen Up: Don't Be Afraid to Hope, Dream, Pray, and Ask God for Your Heart's Desire.
I'm Not Afraid. I Hope. I Dream. I Pray.
I will patiently wait for my desire because I know
God must have more in store in His plans for me.

My Desire: A **R**elationship **I**ntensified by **D**efined **E**nds

Defined/**D**efinitive—Precisely outlined, explicit; being decisive about what you want in a relationship

Why do some people have relationships that don't intensify?

The relationships become:

Deflected:	Something happens to cause them to turn aside, to swerve
Defocused:	Loss of a fixed focus
Deviated:	Turned or moved away from a specified course; to cause to turn aside or differ
Deferred:	Put off until a future time
Delayed:	Postponed until a much later time; to procrastinate, tarry, or linger
Deluded:	Deceived in mind or judgment; not straightforward or honest; to elude or evade
Degraded:	Reduced in rank or status; to lower in morale or intellectual character, to dishonor or disgrace
Deficient:	Lacking an essential quality or element, insufficient

People reach their Comfort Zone and in doing so miss out on the FREEDOM to be themselves.

Reflect on what freedom in a relationship means to you.

What should it feel like? Like knowing your special someone is just a phone call away whenever you need them or to just want to hear their voice. When their physical voice isn't available, just knowing what the person would say or do would be enough to sustain you, to comfort you and force you to look deep inside yourself to feel strong. It should feel intense, making you nervous, excited, and yet calm at the same time . . . a feeling like being lost (in the best possible way) in someone's presence.

Like feeling so good that no matter what you say, what you do, what you think, what you try, what you dream, or if you have a differing opinion, all things are welcome without fear, right?

Someone tell me because I want to feel.

What does this freedom look like? Like peace and serenity. It looks like the sun beating on your face, warming you up. It looks like arms stretched out wide and waiting for one another, then ready to receive when one returns. It looks like arms that are never folded.

Someone tell me because I want to see.

What does it taste like? Like all my favorite fresh fruits: like a sweet peach; like fresh- picked blueberries or strawberries; like watermelon, cantaloupe, or a honeydew—all mixed together. Or, even better, like a bite out of a plump tomato straight from the garden with a dash of salt. Like craving all these things at the same time, even when they're out of season, and knowing that once you've had a taste, you're good to go.

Someone tell me because I want to taste.

What does it smell like? Like cilantro, lemon zest, and dill pickles—all things that make my throat clench before I take my first bite. It smells like my favorite perfumes, like fresh-cut flowers or the aroma of homemade chocolate or a hot fudge sundae on a summer day. It smells like baby powder or a freshly drawn bubble bath.

Someone tell me because I want to smell.

This is the Freedom I Desire.

Are you in your Comfort Zone or in search of your desire or Freedom R.I.D.E.?

The key to finding your freedom is putting your energy into the things you want out of life, into the person who brings out the best in you.

Move on from relationships that are:
Deflected **D**efocused **D**eviated **D**eferred **D**elayed **D**eluded **D**egraded **D**eficient,
As relationships like these may lead to **D**eceit—with people being **D**ishonest or just doing **D**irt.

When you don't reach for FREEDOM, you're not doing anyone a favor.

You are simply discrediting yourself when you disregard your own integrity and self-worth!

BE DEFINITIVE—DEFINE THE QUALITIES YOU WANT IN A RELATIONSHIP AND TELL YOURSELF YOU DESERVE NOTHING LESS.

Define what you want, or you'll be defined by what you settle with.

STEPPING IN BUBBLE GUM

Have you ever been out walking and got gum stuck on your shoe?
Especially when you're on a timeline—Now what do you do?

You try to wipe it off—
You rub your foot across the grass
Only to discover it is sticking way too fast!

You try to use a stick to wipe the gluey gum away
Only to discover it is likely there to stay,

You step back and you think
I've had these shoes a good long while
But they're my favorite pair and, well—
I really like the style.

I don't want to get rid of them—
They're still in good condition.
I'll wear them one more time, I guess,
And then make the transition.

And so, you take that one shoe off
The better to improve
Your chance of cleaning, but you find
Gum's wedged within the groove.

You wash your shoes and dry them
To get then squeaky clean;
The situation's better now—
At least that's how it seems,

Until one day out walking
When you try a different route
You hit a different wad of gum—
Now what is *this* about?

Teresa Lynn Payne

This time the wad is thicker—
You wouldn't ever choose it—
And now each time you take a step
You think you're going to lose it.

You march in place with one foot up
And then down like the other;
The gummy foot gets stuck each time—
Oh, goodness, what a bother!

Just how then to move forward with that gum stuck on your shoe?
You take it off and leave it there . . . *that* is what you do!
You lead off with the other foot, secure in that next rep—
Cause that's the very foot you need to take your next firm step.

HOW COULD IT BE?

How could it be
That God would smile on me
To bring joy to my life
After trials and tribulations,
Relationship woes and strife?

God has a plan, a blueprint, you see,
For women inspired to live their lives free;
To be everything He intends me to be
I need His hands, reshaping me.

How could it be? How will we meet?
A beautiful soul to make my heart beat
A little faster, a lot more intense—
A beautiful dream, but does it make sense?

A man who is gentle, yet strong in his clasp
A man with a vision, with goals in his grasp
A man with integrity, passion for life,
A man who'll look only to God for a wife.

Take the less-traveled road, a barely worn way,
With forks for decisions, at which you must pray.
Move forward and stay on the track;
Make choices going forward and never glance back,

All things have a purpose
Though often disguised
That God will reveal
If we'll open our eyes.

For God has a plan, a blueprint, you see,
For each of us women of God on our knee.
He asks for our buy-in, then answers our prayer:
Unconditional love and a life free from care.

Teresa Lynn Payne

My God has a planned destination for me,
A place filled with peace and a future that's free,
A place without conflict, a life free from sorrow—
I want to move forward, embrace that tomorrow.

My God has a plan for when two people meet
Proceeding in love won't end up in defeat;
Proceeding together builds strength, hope, and faith
KEY ASPECTS, WITH *LOVE*, TO WIN THIS LIFE'S RACE.

So, you say, How Could It Be That God Would Smile on Me?
I know love because God is Love.
> *I know how to love because my family has shown me love.*
> *I know how to give love unconditionally*
> *because I'm blessed to be a mom.*
> *I know what it means to win this race*
> *because I've been running all my life.*
> *I know strength and faith because it's in the*
> *threads of the quilt that my parents built.*

Chapter Seven

TEARDROPS

Isn't it funny that sometimes you feel like crying, sometimes you feel like laughing, sometimes you laugh so hard that you cry, and at other times you've cried so long and hard that you can't laugh because it isn't funny!

—Teresa Lynn

Tears dwell within the soul
The essence of humanity,
The piece that makes us whole.
Deep within emotions surge:
Feelings of happiness, feelings of joy
Feelings of hope and feelings of despair
Feelings that take over when we're not aware
Times when we're anxious, times we're afraid
Times we wish someone would come to our aid
Fighting back tears or just letting tears flow.

Tears come for a reason we seldom control
Tears come when we're overjoyed
Tears come when we're sad
Tears come when we're overwhelmed
And sometimes when we're mad.
Tears show up when we're all alone
Or on a special day, time of year, or season
During a moment when it's time to part
For any type of reason.
Maybe someone is leaving
Maybe there's a special occasion
Maybe a loved one's going on a trip, a break, vacation
Maybe they're only gone for a little while
Or maybe they're not coming back.
Maybe someone has passed away
Maybe someone returns home, safe, sound, and intact.
Tears fall when we get hurt
Tears come when we have pain
Tears come and go but leave their mark,
For we are not the same.
Tears are a source of healing
Bringing comfort to our heart
To help us to regain our strength
To open our ears to what it is the Spirit would impart.
As we share our grief and sorrow
Our happiness and our joy
Jesus gathers our tears and begins to restore
All our disconnected pieces.
He sees each tear that falls
He knows the meaning behind each one
Even before we bow down, cry out, and call,
For God created Tear Drops, and He's our All and All!

BUTTERFLY ON MY SHOULDER

Have you ever lost someone dear to you?
> *Butterfly on my shoulder*
> *Missing piece to my heart . . .*

Felt like you didn't know what to do?
> *Butterfly on my shoulder*
> *Missing piece to my heart*
> *Wishing you were here with me . . .*

Wondered why things happen as they do?
> *Butterfly on my shoulder*
> *Missing piece to my heart*
> *Wishing you were here with me*
> *Hearing words of advice you'd impart . . .*

To love someone deeply—to lose someone young or old
> *Butterfly on my shoulder*
> *Missing piece to my heart*
> *Wishing you were here with me*
> *Hearing words of advice you'd impart*
> *I know that you walk with me . . .*

To not have you here on earth to wonder what the future holds
> *Butterfly on my shoulder*
> *Missing piece to my heart*
> *Wishing you were here with me*
> *Hearing words of advice you'd impart*
> *I know that you walk with me*
> *Whispering in my ear . . .*

A life taken too early saddens me deep within my soul
> *Butterfly on my shoulder*
> *Missing piece to my heart*
> *Wishing you were here with me*
> *Hearing words of advice you'd impart*
> *I know that you walk with me*
> *Whispering in my ear*
> *Words of wisdom and prosperity—guiding me year after year . . .*

I trust the Lord knows what's in store and always takes the best

Butterfly on my shoulder
Missing piece to my heart
Wishing you were here with me
Hearing words of advice you'd impart
I know that you walk with me
Whispering in my ear
Words of wisdom and prosperity—guiding me year after year
Oh, how I love you deeply, oh how I love you so . . .

Even if it shakes me up and puts my faith to the test

Butterfly on my shoulder
Missing piece to my heart
Wishing you were here with me
Hearing words of advice you'd impart
I know that you walk with me
Whispering in my ear
Words of wisdom and prosperity—guiding me year after year
Oh, how I love you deeply, oh how I love you so
Holding fast to cherished memories—never letting go . . .

To hear your voice one more time, to laugh, to shout and sing
Would bring joy to my ears—just hearing your melodious ring

Butterfly on my shoulder
Missing piece to my heart
Wishing you were here with me
Hearing words of advice you'd impart
I know that you walk with me
Whispering in my ear
Words of wisdom and prosperity—guiding me year after year
Oh, how I love you deeply, oh how I love you so
Holding fast to cherished memories—never letting go
But I know you're one of Jesus's sunbeams and that He
loves you so . . .

Looking back over the years
Remembering our last hug and kiss and sigh
Oh, how I long to walk with you
In that sweet by and by.

Teresa Lynn Payne

Butterfly on my shoulder
Whispering in my ear
I feel the presence of the one I love and that I hold so dear.

MY RENDITION OF:

I NEVER KNEW WHY BAD THINGS HAPPEN TO GOOD PEOPLE

I NEVER KNEW
WHY BAD THINGS HAPPEN TO GOOD PEOPLE

To be spared from further or future anguish, illness, or pain

To live or dwell free of aches and pain

To rest and be at peace with the Lord

Knowing their work on earth is done, according to our Father

People have finished their race, fight, or struggle

I NEVER KNEW
WHY BAD THINGS HAPPEN TO GOOD PEOPLE

To open our eyes to see what's missing

To open our hearts and souls to realize it is ourselves that
hold us back from grasping what we need in life

To open our minds

To release trapped destructive messages and negative
thoughts and experiences that hinder us from moving forward

They're a wakeup call like an internal alarm clock telling
us, "It's time to get up, it's time to go, it's time to move."

I NEVER KNEW
WHY BAD THINGS HAPPEN TO GOOD PEOPLE

Teresa Lynn Payne

To grow closer and cherish family, friends, and loved ones

To not take people or life for granted and to bring people closer

To strengthen ties and make amends

To mend broken hearts and heal

I NEVER KNEW
WHY BAD THINGS HAPPEN TO GOOD PEOPLE

A child once told me that bad things happen to good people because no one is perfect.

I NEVER KNEW
WHY BAD THINGS HAPPEN TO GOOD PEOPLE

GOD HAS A PLAN

TO SAVE OUR SOULS

ONLY GOD KNOWS THE WHY.

LOVE, REPENT, FORGIVE, AND HAND OVER YOUR LIFE TO CHRIST

WHILE YOU STILL CAN . . . HE'S PATIENTLY WAITING WITH

OUTSTRETCHED ARMS

Live well today—don't wait for tomorrow. It is not given to you by chance but by God's grace.

—Teresa Lynn

MANY THINGS ABOUT TOMORROW

One of my favorite pastimes is singing songs and singing praise. I'm one of those people who probably sound best singing in the shower or driving down the highway alone in my car, music turned up, or singing with my kids because they think I sound great or just singing in my kitchen while I'm cooking. Anyway, I love music. It's poetry to my ears, rhythm to my feet, and melody for my soul. You can learn a lot from music if you listen beyond the tempo. For some the music makes the song, while for others it's the lyrics that position themselves in their mind, even when they can't hum a note. For me growing up in a little church, full of old gospel hymns, I particularly enjoyed worshipping through song, and I still love to sing praises unto my Savior, my Blessed Assurance whom my faith looks up to for help, health, and favor.

I have one song that has continually entered my mind through various valleys and highpoints in life *(Lord knows I've had plenty)*. The song really transcends our place in this world—a world that we *(no matter what our beliefs may entail)* don't have control over. Everyone should have a life song. My life song that has brought me through valleys to see how God keeps shining through me is a song by Ira Stanphill called "I Know Who Holds Tomorrow."

There's just something about this song that gets me every time I sing it. It soothes my soul.

I Know Who Holds Tomorrow

I don't know about tomorrow
I just live from day to day
I don't borrow from its sunshine
For its skies may turn to grey
I don't worry o'er the future
For I know what Jesus said,

And today I'll walk beside him
For he knows what is ahead

Many things about tomorrow
I don't seem to understand
But I know who holds tomorrow
And I know who holds my hand

Every step is getting brighter
As the golden stairs I climb
Every burden's getting lighter
Every cloud is silver lined
There the sun is always shining
There no tear will dim the eye
At the ending of the rainbow
Where the mountains touch the sky

Many things about tomorrow
I don't seem to understand
But I know who holds tomorrow
And I know who holds my hand

I don't know about tomorrow
It may bring me poverty
But the one who feeds the sparrow
Is the one who stands by me
And the path that is my portion
May be through the flame or flood
But his presence goes before me
And I'm covered in his blood

Many things about tomorrow
I don't seem to understand
But I know who holds tomorrow
And I know who holds my hand.

Chapter Eight

DREAMY

I dream of a place
     Like two bended trees
     All bound together
     Shared roots, shared leaves.
I dream of a place
     Like the sun beats on my face
     Warming and calming
     Soothing to my taste.
I dream of a place
     Like the clouds in the sky
     Relaxing and drifting
     As time passes by.
I dream of a place
     Like the stars at night
     Shining down on me
     With comforting light.
I dream of a place
     Like the butterflies that bloom
     Spreading bright wings
     To negate the gloom.

I dream of a place
    Like the birds in the air
    Flying freely
    No worries or cares.
I dream of a place
    Like water to dry land
    Brings life into existence
    And sustenance at hand.
I dream of a place
    Like the rainbows you see
    A promise in symbol
    From God down to me.
I dream of a place
    As on mountains so high
    Unhindered to shout out
    For echoed reply.
I dream of a place
    Like wildflowers in the field
    Clear paths to the beauty
    That waits as I yield.
I dream of a place
    Like the power of the ocean
    The undertow and the crashing waves
    In ceaseless, steady motion.
I dream of a place
    Like wading in a clear river
    Flowing in one direction
    No time to turn back, too excited to shiver.
I dream of a place
    Like a stone thrown in a placid lake
    Just where the ripples go
    They don't go by mistake.
I dream of a place . . .
    Where I can be—Me!

Teresa Lynn Payne

WHEN?

WHEN the sun comes up and shines through the sky
Brightening the horizon as I, watching, drive by
Taking it all in, just like a deep sigh,
I look at God's creation with no need to ask why.

WHEN beauty abounds for all to see
What God has in store when we ask and believe
He lays the foundation to care for our needs
Requesting our faith, like a small mustard seed.

WHEN our burdens are heavy, He helps us to stand
He knows our all needs, He holds our hand
Just as He feeds the fowl of the air
His palms testify of His love and care,

WHEN a beacon of light illumines the night
Revealing what's hidden, providing insight
Like the glow from a candle that brightens a room
Or softens the moment with peace without gloom.

WHEN smiles abound for all to see
From a ray of light instilled in me
The great joy that resides inside our soul
A healing place—safe to surrender control.

WHEN showers fall down with life's heavy weight
Lift your voice to the heavens, proclaim still your faith
As you kneel to pray and petition God
Give thanks, sing praise, shout out, be proud.

RELATIONSHIP M-A-T-T-E-R-S

Relationships Built on a Good Foundation = 4 Elements:
Spiritual, Intellectual, Social, and Physical
Logical Progression by God's Design:

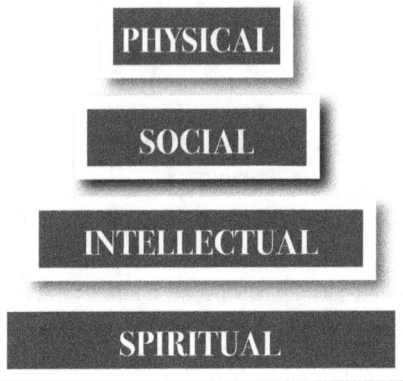

PHYSICAL

SOCIAL

INTELLECTUAL

SPIRITUAL

Relationships with the spiritual element as the foundation are built to withstand and last through time.

Relationships with the physical element as the foundation are built to fall apart due to an unbalanced structure over time.

SPIRITUAL

INTELLECTUAL

SOCIAL

PHYSICAL

Placing emphasis solely on the physical and social elements yields unhealthy progression in relationship building because alone these elements are less meaningful—unable to uphold or support, they make it more difficult to get through any hardship or challenge.

SPIRITUAL: That which is of the Spirit, distinguishing the soul from the body or material matters; Refined in thought and/or feeling; That which is religious and/or in the church; Having a good character, full of spirit, and true; Having an essential quality; The thinking, feeling part of a man or woman, of a spiritual mind.

Seeing each other from a spiritual perspective and starting a relationship with God at the center or your life

Praying to God and looking to Him for direction and guidance and praying together

Imagine yourself as a whole and not the sum of different parts

Risk opening up to someone you're getting to know spiritually for growth and to build trust in the relationship

Include each other when making decisions; talk to one another often with an open heart

Take time to take up your cross daily and worship God together weekly

Undo or release inhibitions you may have; examine your heart, mind, and soul; and open yourself up to be loved unconditionally and to love as God loved us

Always have a forgiving heart and share true intentions

Learn about one another's spiritual foundation and upbringing, share matters of the heart, and talk about your beliefs and values

Spirituality in a relationship from the beginning sets the course for all good things to prosper.

Spirituality in a relationship is taking everything to the Lord in prayer, at first as one and then together.

Matthew 6:33—*But seek ye first the kingdom of God, and his righteousness; and all these things shall be added unto you.*

Philippians 4:19—*But my God shall supply all your needs according to his riches in glory by Christ Jesus.*

INTELLECTUAL: Pertaining to or appealing to the intellect; requiring or involving the intellect; One who is inclined toward intellectual activities; Showing high intelligence; a person having intellectual tastes or work. Intelligence: One's ability to reason and understand and learn from experience; One's ability to respond successfully to new situations.

Inwardly look to the mind of another

Never stop communicating with one another

Talking together daily regarding anything and everything stimulates the brain . . . and you

Every time someone shares something with you—listen closely

Leave negative thoughts and actions and unhealthy spoken words out of the picture

Limit the time you engage in mindless activity

Every now and then dream together; talk about your aspirations, what you want in life

Care for one another by looking out for one another in all matters

Tell that person how much you love them or talk to them about true love or what love is

Unwavering desire to know someone deeply is what to strive for

Always remember that connecting at the mind goes hand-in-hand with a connection of the heart

Liken yourself to a sponge and absorb everything about someone—the good, the bad, the hopes, the dreams, the wins, the losses, the accomplishments, the awards, what saddens them, what excites them, their likes and dislikes, family members loved and lost, special memories as a child, the fears, the desires of the heart, and anything else spoken to you.

Remember—KNOWLEDGE SPEAKS—BUT WISDOM LISTENS

SOCIAL: Living together in a situation or group relation affecting common welfare; Ranks of society; Getting along well with others, sociable; of or for companionship; Engaging in informal gatherings for recreation. Sociable: Friendly; enjoying or requiring the company of others; Characterized by pleasant, informal conversation and companionship.

Setting yourself up to always be surrounded by and engaged in the company of other people

Oftentimes leads to not being comfortable alone or as two—a couple

Caring enough to support and engage in others' interests and functions with families, friends, activities, etc.

Is an important component of relationships

Although social outings and gatherings are not the core of relationship building

Look out for your own self-interest but also the interest of others.

Love to spend time alone with one another—like to be in the company of others

PHYSICAL: Of nature and all matter; of the body, as opposed to the mind; of the flesh versus the spirit; Involving sex and sexuality; Drawn to physical appearances and external attractiveness.

Placing emphasis on outward beauty and acts of sexual intimacy

Has no room for growth—no effort to get to know someone in an intimate way beyond the physical

You must look inside a person and know their heart

Seeing someone to fulfill sexual desires or having someone to show off or display

Is not how relationships last

Clearly a relationship that lacks physical attraction or is void of fulfilling physical needs is dull

Always ask yourself if you would still love someone if you had to lose any part of these physical elements in a mate/partner.

Look to the heart, mind, and spirit first, and all else will come together as one

Colossians 3:2—*Set your affection on things above, not on things of the earth.*

Psalm 37:4—*Delight yourself in the Lord and he will give you the desires of the heart.*

MORE ON RELATIONSHIP M-A-T-T-E-R-S:

Connect through the Spirit with a Spiritual Connection
Tap into the Intellect with Intellectual Wisdom
Enjoy the Social through Social Aims and Determinations
Feel the Physical through Physical Longing and Genuine Attraction.

Stimulate my heart so that I can feel
Stimulate my mind that I may see what's real
Stimulate my well-being and make me whole
Stimulate my body and open my soul.

Do not look to others to do and provide what has already been done and provided for you through Jesus Christ our Lord. In relationships, allow Jesus to be the Provider, the Leader, the Guide, the All-Knowing, the Creator of all, the Way Maker, and the Peace Maker.

Only through God can we learn to love without conditions
Only through God can we learn to forgive
Only through God can we learn to see
Good things will come—just wait and believe.

THE BOWMAKER

The Bible, God's Word, tells us we are valuable. We are created in God's image. We are loved—each one of us. We are so very loved that God sent His Son, Jesus, to make a way for us to be His children.

> **John 3:16—*For God so loved the world that he gave his only begotten son that whosoever believeth in him shall not perish but have everlasting life.***

Yet we don't see ourselves with God's eyes. We see ourselves as plain, basic, unexciting, even in disconnected pieces. It is not hard to believe that we are made from the dust of the earth. We are awaiting the Bowmaker.

We make choices in our lives. We want to be something special— for the God who loves us—for Jesus who died in our place. We try to follow the pattern God shows us—in Jesus—in His Word. Yet our efforts fall so far short even at our best. And sometimes we don't give our best—we don't try, we don't obey—we choose rebellion.

What can we do? The answers are not pleasant or comfortable. The answers don't make sense to our logic:

"Love your enemies"
"Do good to those who despitefully use you"
"Pick up your cross daily"
"Submit"
"Trust."

And God is Faithful
God is worthy of our trust.
God is the potter; we are the clay.
God is the Bowmaker;
We are the paper ribbon.

We begin by allowing God's Word to be the center, the anchor, the tie that binds our heart to Him.

He will even gather those experiences we consider worthless mistakes. He wastes nothing in the lives given to Him.

And we submit to the circumstances God allows to reach our lives: Disappointment—Embarrassment—Failure—Illness or injury—Suffering . . . or even Success.

These circumstances will:
>Twist and pull us
>Wrench our feelings
>Stretch our hearts.

We become what we could never make for ourselves. And that realization opens us to be used in multiple ways we could never have dreamed possible.

God's Spirit brightens us—to be festive in celebration of God's presence in our lives—to be a calm, encouraging support to others.

Having once experienced God's handiwork in our lives—
And within this submission to our God of Love and Faithfulness—

We can even survive those life circumstances that seem
>To destroy us
>To tear us apart
>To unravel us in fear and pain.

Even then God is faithful—God is love—God limits our testing, our trials, to those we can bear.

In His love,
In His presence,
As we submit,
He will remake our lives.

And although we will never be exactly the same,
He will provide a center again.

He will hold us together.
He will gather the disconnected pieces:
He will gently restore us to all we were and
more or to equally beautiful alternatives.

May we be willing to be pliable paper ribbon
in the hands of "The Bowmaker."

Note from the Author: As I began this journey upon graduation from high school, my minister's wife (Lois Hawver) presented me with a gift, a small pink journal that I still cherish today. On the inside cover she wrote the dialogue of "The Bowmaker." She challenged me as I went off to college and as I began my journey into what I call Finer Womanhood & Sisterly Love: to think about the paths I take, to think about the role that God plays in my life at different points in time, and to use the journal to document not only my walk with Christ but how He helps to shape and reshape who I am. Thank you, Lois, for your source of inspiration, through sharing "The Bowmaker" as your gift, and for challenging me to acknowledge God's presence in and through everything.

It is my hope that other women will find their center with the Lord.

1 Corinthians 14:40—*But everything should be done in a fitting and orderly way.*

Romans 8:28—*And we know that in all things God works for the good of those who love him, who have been called according to his purpose.*

I'VE LIVED: I'VE LOVED: AND I'VE BEEN LOVED

I am just a housewife, a mother of 11 loving children and an understanding husband. I feel that I have a special duty to be happy. And happiness does not in any measure depend upon material possessions. I have never been applauded by any big educational speeches, but I have shared with God the wonderful miracles of creation. I've heard tiny voices say you're the bestest murver there is.

Does it matter that I didn't go to college. I have so much to thank God for. Life has not been so easy for me I've had many sicknesses, among them is heart attack, and I thank God I'm here, So what if I don't have a college degree. Once I was told that the greatest university was not found in four walls but in a loving heart an eagerness to help those in need and a willingness to serve God.

Certainly my little part in the great drama of life is small, but we've always been a happy family and when I'm dead the snow will still fall in winter the trees will still bud and put out new life in springtime. Autumn will follow summer and the leaves will drift to the ground as they have done for unnumbered generations, but I feel that I have not lived in vain.

When I'm dead for a little while my children will grieve for me, but I would not have their grief to last long. I would have them think of me as walking the hills in Heaven, greeting old friends and meeting new ones, looking for my share of gold not on the shining streets but in the beautiful blossoming daffodils or the golden rods, happy to be in the presence of my God. I hope to leave a loving family, a host of friends, with a deeper and more sincere faith in God.

I've seen so many people less fortunate than I and so many that never stopped to think or thank the unseen hand of God for what they have. I'm just a housewife, but if I had my life to live over I'd choose it no other way, for I know the rain came before the sunshine, although I did not have too much rain in my life, a few cloudy days and I could soon find sunshine again.

When I'm dead the snow will still fall in winter, the trees will still bud in springtime and put out new life. Autumn will follow summer and the leaves will drift slowly to the ground. For a little time my children will grieve for me. But I would not have their grief to last long. I would have them think of me as walking the Hills of Heaven greeting old friends and meeting new ones, not in the shining streets but among the little ones. Happy to be in the presence of my God.

These words I've written brings pleasure to me. I know some day I'll have to leave, I'll not leave behind no Great Masterpiece but I know I'll leave a host of relatives and friends.

I've lived, I've loved, and I've been loved
Luida
The week of May 10, 1964

Note: My grandma Luida went to the hospital by ambulance on June 4, 1964, and passed on June 5 at 10 a.m. This letter was written by my grandma to her family less than three weeks before her death.

Luida Moore Campbell, of Farmer's Union, North Carolina, is my maternal grandmother. She was a wife to my grandaddy, Slade Campbell. She was the mother of many children and my beautiful mom, Virginia Deloris Campbell Todd, affectionately known as Shag, who is married to my handsome dad, Kenneth Duane Todd of Remus, Michigan. It was not until I read this beautiful letter that my mom shared with me that I realized that my pleasure in writing must be in my genes, like that of my dear grandma whom I didn't have the pleasure to meet. She was driven by the Spirit, and that Spirit drives my mom's same creativity. Along with these two beautiful women, the Spirit and my daddy also drive me.

Teresa Lynn Payne

HOME IS WHERE MY HEART IS

I was searching but could not find it, as hard as I had tried
I found it where I least expected, so surprising I almost cried
But there it was, not far from me, close by for many years
If I knew then what I know now it would have brought me to tears.

Why didn't I see it? Why didn't I know?
Why did I find it now when it was not mine to grow?
Still, . . . when first invited to meet, I knew not what to expect—
How can anyone know what will be next?

I proceeded with caution and anticipation
Like two old souls matched up again without trepidation.

I pulled into the driveway on a snowy night,
Stepped out and walked slowly to the door.
My heart was beating out of my chest—
I could sense this missing part to my core.

The door opened to me—like arms stretched, open wide,
Ready to receive me like two friends embracing
After time and life have passed us by.

But the feelings set in: peace, joy, the laughs within,
Reminiscing on good times too many to group
All coming home to rest on our stoop.

I found my heart that night. How could I live or breathe without it?
How did I think I had it in reach, only to have it broken and
doubt it?

I knew my way there then
To come and go as much as I please
But time would tell soon enough
That a missing part needs one to be complete.

Taking Care of Me

I am that part that is cared for by my heart
My heart is open and makes me a priority—
Always has, ever since I found it—

It is mine. It treats me with care, respect, and love; it knows me.
It sees me. Even when I do not think it knows, . . . it does.

My heart is in tune with me. My heart keeps the door open and the light on,
Shining bright for all to see and know.

My heart does not keep secrets, especially not from me. It does not desire or even think of hiding me, my beauty, or our connection. My heart is part of me. I have entrusted my heart with everything I have. It will not hurt me, let me down, or let anyone else show disrespect for me or us. My heart is true. It cannot be shaken. It is built on a solid foundation. Now I hope for and dream of two hearts. not one.

For it cannot persist and just be on its own—when there's so much lost time and good times ahead to explore in our home.

I am Home and My Heart is there in our home. We can exist. We love, We laugh, We learn from one heart to another.

From my home to our home. Excitement fills the air. Distance does not separate us. Aromas fill the air like something sweet baking in the oven or cooking on the stove, or like fresh flowers in the room, for I know what feeds my heart.

The strength of my heart is like no other. Like a strong tower, my heart is my rock. Solid, dark, fit, and framed to fill up my vessel until I meet my heart and feel it breathing in my chest—my heart lays its ear softly across my chest and listens every time in the stillness of the room or night. It is familiar, and I have often wondered why my heart listens to the rhythm within me. Then it hits me—**My Heart is Home**. Comfortable, cared for, worry-free, loved unconditionally.

Teresa Lynn Payne

It has been running a race trying to catch its own breath, searching to find me—and here I am. This journey called life is what my heart says. We unite under one roof; we are here.

We were not looking but our hearts were.
We were not expecting anything in return, but our souls were.
We were not knowing what to do but our bodies did.
We were not taking anything from our hearts, but we gave ourselves to one another.
We were not pushing each other but pulling for one another in all things.
We were not jumping right in but taking risks and making moves.
We were not talking for the sake of talking but were listening to every word.
We were not just laughing and sharing stories (good, bad, otherwise) but opened ourselves up to be vulnerable.
We were not closed-hearted with one another but trusted with all our might.
We were not just being physical but knowing each other emotionally, intimately, and intellectually.
We were not just going through the motions, but when my heart found his . . .
We were home.

Home is where I first saw you.
Home is where we first embraced.
Home is where we talked deeply.
Home is where I rest my head on your chest and take your pillow.
Home is where I find my strength.
Home is where you take me in.
Home is where I feel your tight grip.
Home is where I do not want to leave.
Home always welcomes me back.
Home is where I am made to feel carefree, to dream, to relax, to live in peace.
Home is where we explore and share our love.
Home is my pleasure and his.
Home is my family.

Home is his family.
Home is our family.
Home is my last chapter of a good—no, great—love story.
I am incredibly happy and find joy in my home.
I have found my home after all these years.

I am on my way to get you.
I pull up to the driveway on a snowy night.
I step out and walk slowly to the door.
My heart is beating out of my chest.
I can sense a missing part of my core.

The door opens . . .
I feel his embrace.
I see his gorgeous eyes and face as the door opens wider to me—
He is my home.
He is my heart.
And home is where my heart is.

Written 8/6/2021, 12:30 a.m.

This last poem, "Home Is Where My Heart Is" *in Taking Care of Me, Today, Tomorrow, for A Lifetime* **is dedicated to Damion D. Payne, who is my home, my heart, my love.**

On January 1, 2022, just after ringing in the New Year, Damion proposed to me, and you know I said Yes! The time between my authoring this poem on my feelings and his surprise proposal to me on January 1, 2022, lies in 12787200 seconds, 213120 minutes, 3552 hours, 148 days, 21 weeks and 1 day, or 4 months and 26 days.

You just never know, . . . but when you do know, hold on for dear life and make every second of every moment count.

Closing Thoughts

THE CENTERPIECE

I am more than a decorative piece to be put on display—I do not see myself as an intended focus of attention that way. I devote myself to being centered on the people and things that are valuable to me and intend to focus much of my attention and time on being there for any family, friend, or others in need. So, if you have ever interacted with me, am I the Centerpiece, or am I One Piece, One Voice, or just Tee?

I have been called many things in life: the Center of Friendships, the Life of the Party, Bestie, Dat's my Girl Right There, Homie, Mom, Felicity . . . I have been called out of my name too, but that does not deserve attention in *Taking Care of Me, Today, Tomorrow, for a Lifetime.*

In this lifetime of mine—do not get it twisted—I do love a wonderful time and to keep the party rollin'. But when the music stops, people pop and drop, and I have been dancing solo, looking for my lifelong partner to Tango—I am a Centerpiece of Love.

Turns out that the yearnings of my heart are poetic, and my soul is filled with the Spirit of Love. Turns out my path in life has not been perfect, but I seek to be loved through all my imperfections. Turns out that, just when I least expected, the love of my life finds me and accepts me just as I am. Turns out

I do not view myself as a writer, but I put forth the songs that are written in my heart that are just waiting to be released and take flight like an erratic butterfly. My love song is shown through the life I live, in the acts of kindness, compassion and caring I give—and, after almost fifty years, in spoken word and finally expressed to my true love.

The written words in these pages are healing and can be used to feed your soul, just as a butterfly needs to drink the sweet nectar from a flower. If I were a butterfly, I would fly all around the world so everyone could delight in all my colorful ways. So. here is where I will spread my wings, release my lyrics, speak my words, sing my song, and share my bread and jelly because this is my jam . . . today, tomorrow, for a lifetime—How sweet it is.

Galatians 6:9—And let us not grow weary of doing good, for in due season we'll reap, if we do not give up.

April 9, 2022, 3:33 a.m.

Signing off until we meet on these pages again, because I have more gifts to bring through word: So keep reading between the lines in life, color outside the lines once in a while, dance till your feet hurt, love like there's no tomorrow, sing like no one is listening, reach as far as you can, work hard and play harder, laugh until you can't laugh no mo'; and, when it's quiet, dream about what you want today, tomorrow, and for a lifetime. Because You— Yeah, You; I'm Talking About All of You—Deserve All the Happiness!

About the Author

Up from the roots of my family tree
Strong ancestors blazing a trail of freedom and victory.

From Africa and Native land I ascend,
From a rich cultural heritage, my story and ethnicity depend.

From the green in my eyes and the curl of my hair
To my highly arched brows, to the smile I wear

To my high cheek bones, to my brown sunskissed tone
To my held-up chin, to the dimples when I grin

To the sound of my voice and my genre of choice
To the curve of my back, to my fondness for fact,

For asserting myself, speaking out for what's right,
Sometimes combatitive, but mostly polite.

A hard worker I am, with a love for all
Willing to help whenever I'm called

A servant leader (respect is a must)
With unwavering faith in God, Whom I trust.

Family and friends call me Tee, Tree, Tree Tree, TB, Reese Cup, and Tee Tee. Growing up, my cousins called me Trrrrunka (rolling the R's), Reese Cup, Rinky, Dreamy, and Green Eyes. My kids call me Ma or the infamous "Hey Ma." Then there're the enemies—we all have had one or two in our lives, who probably call me whatever it is that they call me. I used to hear my dad say, *"You can call me what you want but don't call me out my name."* I'm going to have to cosign that phrase.

I'm Teresa Lynn Todd. I was born in Grand Rapids, Michigan, to Kenneth Duane Todd and Virginia Deloris (Campbell) Todd of Farmer's Union, North Carolina. I started elementary school on the southeast side of Grand Rapids at Ottawa Hills Elementary. I was raised for most of my growing up years in Remus, Michigan, with two siblings, Marcus O'Neal Todd of Remus and Chandra Tameia Todd, who passed away in 1981 from terminal brain cancer. I gradudated from Chippewa Hills High School. The good Lord taketh and the good Lord giveth: we were blessed in our home with the presence of two high-school exchange students who became family—Takaka Ebara Nishiyama from Japan and José Muro from Spain. Thanks, Mom and Dad, for giving us a brother and a sister.

I received a Bachelor of Science degree in Public Health Education and Health Promotion from Central Michigan University in Mt. Pleasant, Michigan, and a Masters of Health Administration from Grand Valley State University in Grand Rapids. I reside in Byron Center, Michigan with the love of my life, my husband Damion Payne, whom I first met over 30 years ago and reconnected in 2020. I previously lived in Wyoming, Michigan, for twenty-plus years, where I raised my two children. Yes, one of my biggest joys in life is being the mother of two wonderful, intelligent, creative, fun, and loving kiddos, now young adults but still my babies: Dennis Wellington Branson II and Shayna Lynn Branson. I've been blessed with a daughter-in-law, Aubryana Nicole (Swindall) Branson, and my first granddaughter Malaney Amara Branson. Through marriage, I have gained three more family members to love, Octavia Hubert, Kellen, and Cameron Payne

As I come to this moment in sharing my collection of poetry and my story in song, I do it from a new and different state of heart and mind, from the backdrop of a new relationship and a new place to unwind. I'm in the comfort of my new dwelling place with my best friend and love Damion . . . and so my journey continues, as does my bookend.

I began my journey of writing poetry at a very young age and wrote more in-depth as I entered my post-graduate years and my mid-years on the back side of forty (you know what I'm talking about . . . those years when we're busy with work, family, friends, church, school events, and what have you, but not really dwelling on the mundane happenings occurring around us). In the midst of it all, when you least expect it, . . . *LifeThrows You A Curve Ball—Whether You're Ready or Not.*

It's with hope and anticipation that I share my writing.

It's my vision that you will find something that taps you within, that pricks your heart or opens your soul.

It's my desire that something you read will inspire you and that you will share the inspiration with individuals within your sphere of influence, with family and friends, or pass this on as a gift to someone whom you have great hopes and dreams for.

It's my mission that you will not stop at the beginning of this collation of poetry and writing but that you will be sustained through to the end.

It's part of my innate being that my endeavors, goals, and dreams must start with the end in mind. I encourage you to search your soul as well, that you too will realize that the end is just the foundation for a new beginning that will last Today, Tomorrow, and for a Lifetime.

www.ingramcontent.com/pod-product-compliance
Lightning Source LLC
LaVergne TN
LVHW051423080426
835508LV00022B/3213